# I. Introduction

U.S. antitrust law treats exclusive contracts, which require that a buyer make all of its purchases of a particular good from a single seller, under a rule of reason standard in which possible economic efficiencies are balanced against possible anticompetitive harm. "Chicago School" scholars (Richard A. Posner (1976, p. 212) and Robert H. Bork (1978, p. 309)), however, have argued that U.S. antitrust law should treat exclusive contracts as per se legal. They first note that the excluding firm imposes harm on consumers equal to its monopoly profit plus some deadweight loss. They then assume that the excluding firm can not get buyers to sign exclusive contracts except by fully compensating buyers for this harm. Given this assumption, they note that, since the excluding firm only gains the monopoly profit from using exclusive contracts, the excluding firm can not profitably induce buyers to sign exclusive contracts. Based on this, they conclude that efficiency considerations, rather than anticompetitive motives, explain the use of exclusive contracts.

In arguing that exclusive contracts are unlikely to be anticompetitive, the Chicago School model implicitly assumes that buyers are final consumers rather than competing downstream firms and that a buyer does not impose externalities on other parties when it signs an exclusive contract. This paper shows that when these two assumptions are relaxed, an upstream incumbent monopolist can often use exclusive contracts to deter entry. Unlike several previous papers (e.g., Eric B. Rasmusen et al. (1991), Illya R. Segal & Michael D.Whinston (2000a)), we show that this is true even where upstream scale economies are absent.

In this paper, we consider a model where an entrant can not initially supply a buyer at the same cost as the incumbent monopolist. This condition would hold if "learning by doing"

1

enabled upstream firms to produce at lower cost over time. It would also hold if downstream firms required some period of testing before they would commit to obtain a substantial portion of their inputs from a new entrant. Next, we assume that this entrant can supply buyers with the input at the same cost as the incumbent firm after the initial period as long as exclusive contracts have not shut it out of the industry. Exclusive contracts can do this if they preclude the incumbent from producing in the initial period, thereby preventing "learning by doing"[1] or product testing.

Given these assumptions, the incumbent firm can create a prisoner's dilemma for the downstream firms by offering these firms discounts for signing an exclusive contract. A downstream buyer that refuses to sign the exclusive contract foregoes the discount. Foregoing the discount puts the non-signing firm at a cost disadvantage relative to any downstream competitor that signs the exclusive contract. As a consequence, the non-signing firm loses profit to the signing firm(s) during the interim period. When the entrant comes in, both the non-signing firm and the signing firms obtain the upstream good at a duopoly price. This increases the profits of both the non-signing firm and the signing firms equally over their pre-entry profits. In this payoff structure it is profitable for the incumbent to offer a discount such that all downstream firms sign the exclusive contract even though, over the long-term, they would obtain the upstream good at a lower price and earn a higher profit if they all refused to sign. Thus, the incumbent monopolist can use exclusive contracts to deter efficient entry.

We also consider a slight variation of the above model where the entrant does not exist in

---

[1]The entrant may not be able learn without a buyer since what it needs to learn may be something specific to the industry that only a buyer can provide.

period 1 but can produce the input at the same cost and at the same scale as the incumbent in period 2. In this model, the incumbent monopolist can use its control over period 1 input prices to induce downstream firms to pay it a monopoly price in period 2 *if* it can use long-term contracts. Specifically, instead of requiring that buyers agree to only buy from the incumbent in the first period, the incumbent requires buyers to sign exclusive contracts that force them to purchase only from the incumbent in the second period. In order to create the prisoner's dilemma for the downstream competitors, the contract must ensure that a downstream firm that signs the contract does not pay a higher input price than any firms that do not sign the contract if entry occurs. This can be accomplished either by a price matching clause or by committing to supply the input at or near cost whenever not all downstream competitors have signed the exclusive contract.[2] With such a contract, the logic of the original model guarantees that there will be a first period discount for exclusive dealing that will induce all firms to sign the contract, eliminating any market for the entrant's product (see Section V).

This type of contract can also be thought of as a tying agreement where the tie is across periods. If the incumbent produced two (not completely complementary) products that are both used by competing downstream firms, a similar tying agreement between the two products would profitably exclude competition in one market. Thus, the model not only shows that exclusive contracts can profitably deter entry when an incumbent is selling to downstream competitors, it also shows that tying contracts can be both anticompetitive and profitable in this circumstance as well.

---

[2]Note, neither the price matching clause nor the ability to commit to a future price (at or above cost) will alone deter entry since there is no entry cost. The exclusive contract is necessary for entry deterrence.

Three critical differences between our basic model and that of the Chicago School generate the entry deterring effect of exclusive contracts. The first is that we allow the incumbent monopolist to compensate the buyers for signing the exclusive contract through lower unit prices rather than just lump-sum transfers. As a result, the cost of the compensation to the incumbent is less than the benefit to the buyers (lower prices reduce the dead weight loss). Second, our model is a multi-period model rather than a one-period model. The monopolist has a period to reward (punish) buyers who sign (do not sign) the exclusive contract during which a non-signer cannot reap the benefits of competition. Third, as mentioned above, the Chicago School model assumes that there are no externalities among buyers. In contrast, we assume that the buyers are competing against each other in a downstream market. Thus, when one buyer pays a higher unit price for the product, other buyers have a competitive advantage in that market. This gives the incumbent an extra way to reward (punish) buyers for signing (not signing) the exclusive contract. Essentially, it can force a non-signing buyer to bear some of the cost of compensating a signer for signing the contract.

By relaxing the Chicago School's assumption that a buyer does not impose externalities on other parties when it signs an exclusive contract, several recent papers have also shown that an incumbent monopolist can use exclusive contracts to deter entry. Rasmusen et. al. (1991) and Segal and Whinston (2000a) show that exclusion can be profitable assuming the following: 1) an incumbent monopolist sells to diffuse buyers; 2) a potential entrant would need to make sales to more than one buyer; and 3) a potential entrant's minimum viable scale is large relative to industry sales.[3] In these papers, buyers who sign exclusive contracts prevent the entrant from attaining its minimum viable scale. This, in turn, imposes an externality on buyers who do not sign exclusive contracts. Our paper is similar to these papers in that we also rely on externalities to show that exclusive contracts can deter entry. Our paper differs from these papers in that we show an incumbent monopolist can use exclusive contracts to deter entry even in the absence of scale economies.

B. Douglas Bernheim and Whinston (1998) consider a model with the following assumptions: 1) a single market is served by a single retailer; 2) with time, a second retail market becomes viable; and 3) a manufacturer must serve more than one market to achieve important scale economies. Given these assumptions, Bernheim and Whinston show that in certain circumstances a manufacturer can gain a monopoly in the second retail market by signing an exclusive contract with the first retailer. Thus, in the Bernheim and Whinston model, a manufacturer and the first retailer form a coalition to extract monopoly profit from the second retailer. As with the Rasmusen et al. and Segal and Whinston papers, the Bernheim and Whinston paper relies on the assumption that an upstream firm must make sales to more than one buyer in order to obtain important scale economies. As noted above, our paper does not make this assumption.

Finally, Phillippe Aghion and Patrick Bolton (1986) consider a model with the following assumptions: 1) an incumbent monopolist sells to a single buyer; 2) absent exclusive contracts, a

---

[3]For example, assume that an incumbent monopolist sells to 100 buyers of equal size, and that this incumbent, by signing exclusive contracts with 61 buyers, can prevent an entrant from attaining its minimum viable scale. Given these assumptions, exclusion would be profitable if the monopoly profit from all 100 buyers exceeded the required compensation to 61 buyers.

new seller would enter if it had lower costs than the incumbent; 3) absent exclusive contracts, this entrant would gain as surplus the difference between his cost of production and the incumbent's cost of production. Given these assumptions, Aghion and Bolton note that the incumbent monopolist and the buyer can sign a contract with liquidating damages that would force the entrant to pay some of his surplus to the incumbent/buyer coalition. While this would sometimes deter efficient entry, the incumbent/buyer coalition only benefits from the exclusive contract when entry actually occurs. To get this result, the Aghion and Bolton model relies on the assumption that the entrant has lower costs than the incumbent. In contrast, our model explains the use of exclusive contracts when the incumbent and the entrant have similar costs.

The remainder of this paper is organized as follows: Section II presents a simple two period model in which an incumbent monopolist can profitably use exclusive contracts to deter entry. Section III extends this result to the infinite horizon case. Section IV considers whether an entrant can successfully counter the incumbent monopolist's use of exclusive contracts. Section V analyzes the basic model assuming that both the incumbent and entrant can sign long-term contracts, and Section VI concludes.

## II. Simple Two-Period Model

Our model relies on the following assumptions:

1. There are two periods, with no discounting.

2. An upstream monopolist[4] (the incumbent) sells to two downstream competitors.

3. Entry requires no fixed cost, but in the first period in which it enters, an entrant's production must be very small (so that buyers can test its product).

4. If the entrant can make sales in period 1, then in period 2 the entrant can produce at the same cost as the incumbent. Thus, the entrant can attain his minimum viable scale in period 2 by selling to a single downstream firm in period 1.

The sequence of actions is the following:

1. The upstream monopolist offers downstream buyers a choice between a non-exclusive contract at the monopoly price or an exclusive contract that offers a discounted price for purchases in period 1.[5]

2. The downstream firms independently decide which contract to accept.

Because of assumption (3), in the entrant's first period of existence the incumbent's myopically optimal strategy is to price at the monopoly level. Thus, if both downstream firms sign the exclusive contract, then the incumbent sells to them at the discounted price in period 1

---

[4]Throughout this paper, we use the term monopolist as shorthand for a dominant firm.

[5]While, this may not be the optimal form for the exclusive contract, we only need to show that there exists an exclusive contract that can profitably deter entry.

and charges them the monopoly price in period 2. If one of the downstream firms refuses to sign the exclusive contract, then, in period 1, the monopolist sells to the signer at the discounted price and sells to the non-signer at the monopoly price. (This contract is renegotiation proof since, in period 1, the entrant's low production (assumption 3) ensures that the monopolist's best response to entry is to charge the non-signer the monopoly price.[6]) In period 2, the entrant and the monopolist compete in some duopoly pricing game yielding a price somewhere in between marginal cost and the monopoly price.

Define: $\pi_m =$ the downstream firm's profit when it and its competitor pay a monopoly upstream price.

$\pi_D =$ the downstream firm's profit when it and its competitor pay a discounted monopoly price to the upstream firm.

$\pi_h =$ the downstream firm's profit when it pays a discounted monopoly price to the upstream firm and its competitor pays the monopoly price.

$\pi_l =$ the downstream firm's profit when it pays the monopoly price to the upstream firm and its competitor pays a discounted price.

$\pi_e =$ the downstream firm's profit when entry creates upstream duopoly competition.

Thus, the payoffs for the downstream firms are as follows. If both downstream firms sign exclusive contracts with discounts, then both downstream firms earn $\pi_D$ in the first period and $\pi_m$

---

[6]It is possible that the non-signer's demand curve is slightly altered when the signer receives the input at the discounted price, thus changing the optimal monopoly price for that consumer. As will become clear, taking this into account would not affect the results.

in the second period. If neither downstream firm signs an exclusive contract then an entrant

enters in period 1, and both downstream firms earn $\pi_m$ in period 1 and $\pi_e$ in period 2. If one firm

signs the exclusive and one does not, then an entrant enters in period 1, and the signer earns $\pi_h$ in

period 1 and $\pi_e$ in period 2. The non-signer earns $\pi_l$ in period 1 and $\pi_e$ in period 2. These

payoffs are related as follows:

(1) $$\pi_e > \pi_m > \pi_l \text{ and } \pi_h > \pi_D > \pi_m > \pi_l$$

Downstream firms earn greater profits when both can buy their inputs at the duopoly

price than at the monopoly price. A downstream firm earns more profits when it can buy the

input at a discounted price while its rival has to pay the monopoly price than when both get the

discounted price (this is due to the fact that these firms are competitors). When both get the

input at the discounted price, however, they each earn greater profits then when both have to pay

the monopoly price. And, a firm earns more profits when both pay the monopoly price than

when it pays the monopoly price while its rival gets a discount (again, due to competition). We

will show below that the discounted price will be weakly greater than the duopoly price, so $\pi_e >$

$\pi_D$, but this is not an assumption of the model.

Given these payoffs, the following prisoner's dilemma game represents the situation faced by the downstream firms when deciding whether or not to sign the exclusive contract.

|  |  | downstream firm 2 | |
| --- | --- | --- | --- |
|  |  | sign | don't sign |
| downstream | sign | $\pi_D + \pi_m$, $\pi_D + \pi_m$ | $\pi_h + \pi_e$, $\pi_l + \pi_e$ |
| firm 1 | don't sign | $\pi_l + \pi_e$, $\pi_h + \pi_e$ | $\pi_m + \pi_e$, $\pi_m + \pi_e$ |

payoffs to: (downstream firm 1, downstream firm 2)

For each downstream firm, signing the exclusive contract is a dominant strategy as long as the following conditions hold:

Condition 1: $\pi_h + \pi_e \geq \pi_m + \pi_e$ or $\pi_h \geq \pi_m$

This condition requires that the downstream firm's profit when it gets a discount and its competitor pays the monopoly price exceeds its profit when both it and its competitor pay the monopoly price. This condition holds for any positive discount.

Condition 2: $\pi_D + \pi_m \geq \pi_l + \pi_e$ or $\pi_m - \pi_l \geq \pi_e - \pi_D$

Since $\pi_m - \pi_l$ is positive, $\pi_e - \pi_D$ can also be positive. This, in turn, implies that the downstream firms' profits with the discount can be less than their profits with duopoly. That is, the

10

incumbent monopolist's discounted price can exceed the duopoly price.

Finally, offering the exclusive contracts with the discount is profitable for the incumbent monopolist as long as his profit with the discount exceeds his profit with duopoly.

Condition 3: $\pi_{I,D} \geq \pi_{I,d}$

This condition holds because, as noted above, downstream firms will accept a discounted price that exceeds the duopoly price. Thus, we have proved the following result.

*Proposition 1. Whenever there is some competition between the two downstream firms (i.e., payoffs are given by (1)), then the monopolist can profitably offer a discount for signing an exclusive contract that both downstream firms will sign, and, thus, deter entry.*

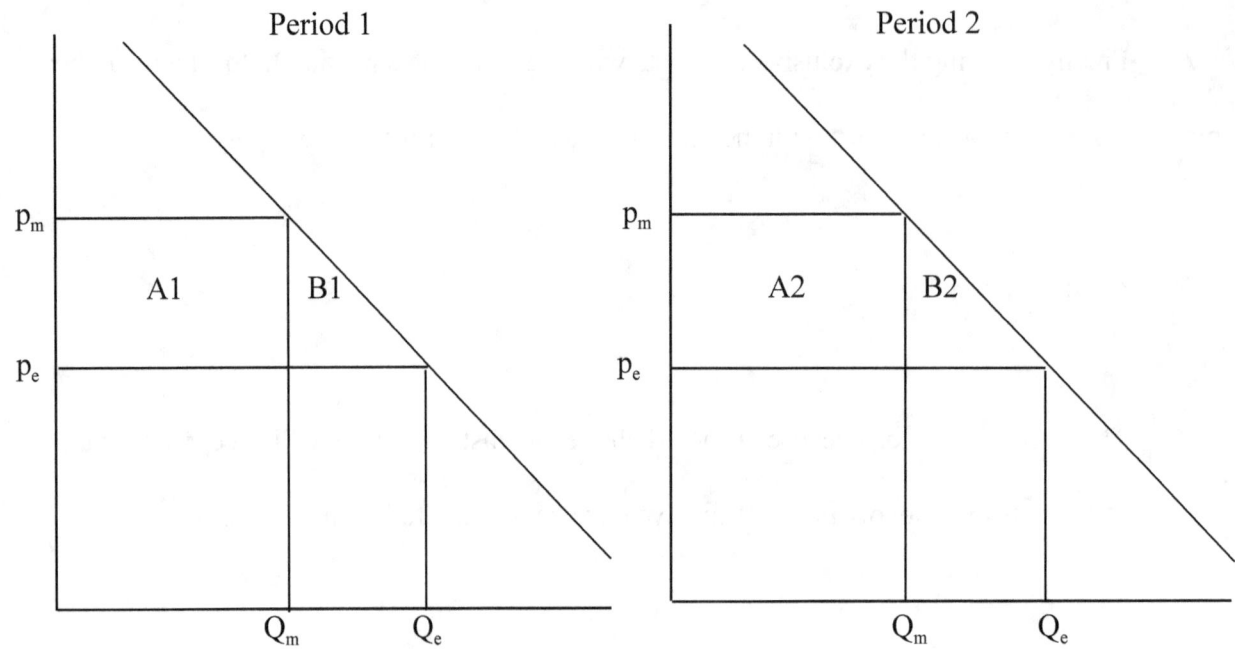

To give some intuition to our model, it is useful to return to the basic argument of Posner and Bork. The figure on the left shows the upstream market in period 1, and the figure on the right shows the upstream market in period 2. Let us assume for now that downstream buyers do not compete at all. Posner and Bork argue that an incumbent monopolist in period 1 could only get buyers to sign exclusive contracts by offering to compensate them for the area A2 + B2. However, according to Posner and Bork, this would be unprofitable for the monopolist because it only obtains A2 by using exclusive contracts.

This analysis, however, overlooks an important feature of this two period model: The incumbent monopolist is in a unique position to compensate buyers for signing exclusive contracts. By lowering its prices in period 1 from the monopoly price to the price after entry (the duopoly price), the monopolist can compensate the buyers an amount A1 + B1 at a cost of only

A1 to itself. Thus absent competition among downstream buyers, the monopolist can offer downstream buyers who sign exclusive contracts a discount equal to the difference between the monopoly price and the duopoly price. This would fully compensate downstream buyers for their second period losses without imposing overall (period 1 + period 2) losses on itself. Essentially, the incumbent deters entry by giving the buyers a period of duopoly pricing and a period of monopoly pricing (exactly what they would get with entry) if they sign the exclusive contract.

Let us now add downstream competition. With downstream competition, a downstream firm with lower costs than its rival earns more profit than its rival for two reasons: It has lower costs, and these lower costs enable it to capture a disproportionate amount of market share at the expense of its rival. Consequently, the desire to gain market share at its rival's expense and to prevent its rival from gaining market share at its expense gives downstream competitors a strong incentive to sign an exclusive contract and obtain a discount. For this reason, even a small amount of downstream competition would enable the monopolist to get downstream firms to sign exclusive contracts even when it offers them a discount that leaves its first period price above the duopoly level.

Of course, the amount of anticompetitive harm from the use of exclusive contracts in this model depends on the size of this discount. If the discount is very large (the first period price is close to the duopoly level), then the anticompetitive harm from using exclusive contracts to deter entry is comparatively small. If the discount is small (the first period price is close the monopoly level), then the anticompetitive harm from using exclusive contracts to deter entry will be larger. As we discussed above, when the downstream firms do not compete at all, exclusive contracts can deter entry, but they do not affect the total input prices paid by the downstream buyers (they

13

only reverse the periods when monopoly and duopoly prices are paid). If the downstream firms engage in Bertrand competition (with undifferentiated products), however, the incumbent can come arbitrarily close to the monopoly outcome in both periods. This occurs because the downstream buyers do not care at all about the level of the input price, only its relation to the input price paid by their rival. So, they both earn zero profits in period 2 whether there is entry or not (since both pay the same input prices in that period). Thus, each buyer will sign the exclusive contract for any arbitrarily small discount.

Whether this relationship between downstream competition and the size of the discount holds everywhere is more problematic. The incumbent will offer an exclusive contract with a discount that meets Condition 2 with equality:

(2) $$\pi_D + \pi_m = \pi_l + \pi_e$$

or

(2*) $$(\pi_e - \pi_D) - (\pi_m - \pi_l) = 0$$

We now rewrite $\pi_m$ and $\pi_e$ as a function of downstream competition $(\theta)$ and rewrite $\pi_D$ and $\pi_l$ as a function of both downstream competition $(\theta)$ and the size of the discount $(D)$:

(2**) $$(\pi_e (\theta) - \pi_D (\theta,D)) - (\pi_m (\theta) - \pi_l (\theta,D)) = 0$$

Differentiating (2**) with respect to $\theta$ gives the following

(3) $$0 = \{\partial(\pi_e (\theta) - \pi_D (\theta,D))/\partial\theta - \partial(\pi_m (\theta) - \pi_l (\theta,D))/\partial\theta\} - (\partial D/\partial\theta)[\partial( \pi_D (\theta,D) - \pi_l (\theta,D))/\partial D]$$

which can be rewritten as:

(4) $$(\partial D/\partial\theta) = \{\partial(\pi_e (\theta) - \pi_D (\theta,D))/\partial\theta - \partial(\pi_m (\theta) - \pi_l (\theta,D))/\partial\theta\} / \partial( \pi_D (\theta,D) - \pi_l (\theta,D))/\partial D$$

The denominator of this expression, $(\partial(\pi_D (\theta,D) - \pi_l (\theta,D))/\partial D)$, is positive. A larger discount increases a firm's profit when both it and its rival get the discount but reduces a firm's

14

profit when its rival gets the discount but it does not. The first term in the numerator $(\partial(\pi_e(\theta) - \pi_D(\theta,D))/\partial\theta)$ is negative. As downstream competition intensifies, the benefit to a firm from getting an input at the duopoly price rather than the higher discounted monopoly price is competed away.

The sign of the second term in the numerator $(\partial(\pi_m(\theta) - \pi_l(\theta,D))/\partial\theta)$ is more problematic. Certainly, starting from the point of no competition (the two products are unrelated) the sign must be positive since increasing the degree of downstream competition must increase the difference $\pi_m(\theta) - \pi_l(\theta,D)$. (This difference is zero when the products are unrelated since my rival's output price (and, thus input price) does not affect my profits, but is positive when there is some competition.) When the two products become very close substitutes, however, this sign may be negative. If the firm paying the lower input price chooses to price at the marginal cost of the firm paying the higher input price, then increased competition would have no effect on $\pi_l(\theta,D)$, while continuing to reduce $\pi_m(\theta)$.

If the second term in the numerator were always positive, then the total expression would always be negative. This would imply that the discount that the incumbent must pay falls as downstream competition intensifies. However, because the second term will sometimes be negative, we cannot rule out the possibility that, for some downstream demand functions, there is a region where greater downstream competition does not reduce the required discount. That said, we conjecture that such regions either only exist for very peculiar demand functions or do not exist at all.

## III.  An Infinite Horizon Model

In this section, we show that the main results of the two period model are still valid in an infinite horizon setting.  We assume that the entrant can enter at any period and that long term exclusive contracts are not feasible.  As was true above, if exclusive contracts deter entry in this case, they will still deter entry when the menu of possible exclusive contracts is expanded.  We now introduce a discount rate, $\beta$ and let $V$ represent the downstream firm's value function.  This value function will depend only on whether or not there is a fully qualified entrant (an entrant that has already had one period of (tiny) sales).  As before, Condition 1 always holds.  The analogue of Condition 2  requires that in any no entry state (NE), a downstream firm will sign an exclusive when its rival has signed the exclusive.  That is:

Condition 2′:  $\pi_D + \beta * V(NE) \geq \pi_I + \beta * V(E)$  or  $\pi_D - \pi_I \geq \beta * (V(E) - V(NE))$

(We allow the discount in this model to differ from the discount in any prior model.)  If the incumbent monopolist finds it profitable to offer a discount that satisfies this condition in any given period, it will find it profitable to do so in every period.  Thus, one can write the previous expression as follows:

(5) $\qquad\qquad \pi_D - \pi_I \geq (\beta / 1 - \beta) * (\pi_e - \pi_D)$  or  $\pi_D \geq \beta * \pi_e + (1 - \beta) * \pi_I$

From this, it is easy to see that as the discount factor increases (it takes the entrant less time to be able to compete with the incumbent on an equal footing) the required discount must increase.  In the limit, as the discount factor approaches one, the incumbent must offer the downstream firms duopoly prices to get them to continue to agree to the exclusive contract.

Finally, offering the exclusive contracts with the discount is profitable for the incumbent monopolist as long as his profit with the discount exceeds his profit with duopoly.

Condition 3': $(1/1-\beta)\ \pi_{I,D} \geq \pi_{I,m} + (\beta/1-\beta)*\pi_{I,d}$ or $\pi_{I,D} \geq (1-\beta)*\pi_{I,m} + \beta*\pi_{I,d}$

The following proposition shows that exclusive contracts can still deter entry in this infinite-horizon setting.

*Proposition 2.  As long as the downstream market is characterized by some degree of competition, it is profitable for the incumbent to offer a discount for an exclusive contract that deters entry.*

Before proving this result, we first establish the following lemma.

*Lemma 1.  The discount necessary to induce the downstream firms to sign the exclusive is increasing in the discount factor.*

Proof.  Differentiating (5) at equality and rearranging terms gives the following:

(6)          $\partial p_D/\partial \beta = (\pi_e - \pi_I)/[-(1-\beta)\pi_2(p_m,p_D)+(\pi_1(p_D,p_D) +\pi_2(p_D,p_D))]$

Here (and in the proof of Proposition 2), the $\pi$ function with two arguments is the profit of the downstream firm where the first argument is the input price it is paying and the second is the input price its rival pays.  Numerical subscripts on this function represent partial derivatives.

Hence, $\pi_2(p_m,p_D)$ is the derivative with respect to the rival's input price of the profit of the downstream firm when he is paying the monopoly price for the input and his rival is paying the discounted price. The denominator is negative since increasing the discounted price increases the profit of a firm whose rival is paying that price when he is not, and increasing the price both downstream firms pay reduces their profits. The numerator is positive by (1). So, if the discounted price is decreasing in the discount factor, the discount is increasing. Q.E.D.

Proof of Proposition 2. We can rewrite condition 3′ making the dependence of profits on price explicit as follows:

(7) $$\pi_1(p_D)-((1-\beta)*\pi_1(p_m) + \beta*\pi_1(p_e)/2)>0$$

Here, $p_D$ represents the discounted price, $p_e$ the post-entry (duopoly) price, and $p_m$ the monopoly price. $\pi_1$ is the function that gives total upstream profits for a given price. Thus, in the duopoly case I divide by two since the incumbent only gets half the upstream profits after entry.

However, if the following inequality holds then so will (7):

(7*) $$\pi_1(p_D)-((1-\beta)*\pi_1(p_m) + \beta*\pi_1(p_e))>0$$

Differentiating the left hand side of (7*) with respect to $\beta$ gives the following:

(8) $$(\partial p_D/\partial\beta)\ \pi_1{'}(p_D)+\pi_1(p_m) -\pi_1(p_e)$$

Substituting the explicit expression for $\partial p_D/\partial\beta$ obtained in Lemma 1 into the above expression gives the following:

(9) $$\{[\pi(p_e,p_e) -\pi(p_m,p_D)]\ \pi_1{'}(p_D)-(\pi_1(p_m) -\pi_1(p_e))[(1-\beta)\pi_2(p_m,p_D)-(\pi_1(p_D,p_D) +\pi_2(p_D,p_D))]\}$$
$$\{1/[-(1-\beta)\pi_2(p_m,p_D)+(\pi_1(p_D,p_D) +\pi_2(p_D,p_D))]\}$$

The denominator in (9) is negative (it is just the denominator of $\partial p_D/\partial \beta$). To determine the sign

of the numerator we first rewrite it as follows:

(10) $\qquad \{[\pi(p_e,p_e) -\pi(p_m,p_m)+\pi(p_m,p_m)-\pi(p_m,p_D)] \pi_1'(p_D)-(\pi_1(p_m) -\pi_1(p_e))$
$\qquad\qquad [(1-\beta)\pi_2(p_m,p_D)-(\pi_1(p_D,p_D)+\pi_2(p_D,p_D))]\}$

Now, we make the following Taylor's approximations:

$\qquad\qquad \pi(p_e,p_e) -\pi(p_m,p_m) \approx -(p_m-p_e)(\pi_1(p_D,p_D) +\pi_2(p_D,p_D))$
(11) $\qquad\qquad \pi(p_m,p_m)-\pi(p_m,p_D) \approx -(p_m-p_D)\pi_2(p_m,p_D)$
$\qquad\qquad \pi_1(p_m) -\pi_1(p_e) \approx -(p_m-p_e)\pi_1'(p_D)+\pi_1(p_e)$

With these approximations, the numerator simplifies to the following:

(12) $\qquad\qquad\qquad \pi_1'(p_D)\pi_2(p_m,p_D)\{p_e- p_{D+}\beta\ (p_m-p_e)\}$

This expression has the sign of the term in curly braces (so long as $\pi_2(p_m,p_D)>0$, which is true

whenever the two downstream firms compete to some degree). Since $\partial p_D/\partial \beta <0$, this term is

decreasing in $\beta$. At $\beta=0$ it is negative since $p_e<p_D$. As $\beta \to 1$ it is positive since (5) guarantees that

$p_D \to p_e$ when $\beta \to 1$. Thus, for small values of $\beta$, (7) is increasing in $\beta$, while for large values it is

decreasing in $\beta$. Thus, (7) must reach its minimum at either $\beta=0$ or $1$. At $\beta=0$, (7) is zero since

Condition 2″ says that $p_D=p_m$ in this case. Similarly, as $\beta \to 1$ it approaches zero since Condition

2″ says that $p_D \to p_e$ in that case. So, for any possible value of $\beta$, the monopolist can do at least as

well by offering an exclusive contract and deterring entry as by acquiescing to entry. Q.E.D.

## IV. Entrant Counter-Strategies[7]

In this section, we consider whether an incumbent monopolist can use exclusive contracts to increase overall prices in cases where a prospective entrant can make side payments to a downstream firm for refusing to sign the exclusive contract. In considering this, we focus on cases where the incumbent monopolist's discounted price equals or exceeds the duopoly price, since the incumbent actually increases welfare if it offers a discount below the duopoly price.

The maximum side payment that the entrant will offer is its (duopoly) profit after entry in period 2, $\pi_{E,e}$. If the entrant can make sales in period 1, it can compete on an equal footing with the incumbent in period 2. Thus, $\pi_{E,e} = \pi_{I,e}$. Given this, the various conditions become:

Condition 1″: $\pi_h + \pi_e \geq \pi_m + \pi_e + \pi_{I,e}$ or $\pi_h \geq \pi_m + \pi_{I,e}$

Condition 2″: $\pi_D + \pi_m \geq \pi_l + \pi_e + \pi_{I,e}$ or $\pi_m - \pi_l \geq \pi_e - \pi_D + \pi_{I,e}$

Condition 3″: $\pi_{I,D} \geq \pi_{I,e}$

If the monopolist can strictly deter entry with a discount price equal to the post entry price, then it can deter entry with a slightly larger discounted price (slightly smaller discount). Thus, if the monopolist offers a discount price equal the duopoly price, Condition 2″ becomes $\pi_m - \pi_l \geq \pi_{I,e}$. Notice that if Condition 2″ holds in this case, Condition 1″ ($\pi_h - \pi_m \geq \pi_{I,e}$) also (strictly) holds. This follows because total profits of downstream firms will be at least as large when one firm gets a discount as when neither firm gets a discount. Thus, $\pi_h + \pi_l > \pi_m + \pi_m$, which can be

---

[7]See Robert Innes and Richard J. Sexton (1994) and Ilya R. Segal and Michael D. Whinston (2000b) for discussions of counter-strategies that entrants can use in the exclusion theories discussed earlier.

rewritten as $\pi_h - \pi_m > \pi_m - \pi_l$ which is greater than $\pi_{l,e}$ by Condition 2″. Condition 3″ will also hold (strictly, so long as duopoly profits are positive) since we are restricting ourselves to cases where the incumbent's discounted price equals or exceeds the duopoly price. Given this, if a prospective entrant can make side payments to a downstream firm, the incumbent can strictly deter entry and decrease social welfare if and only if:

(13) $$\pi_m - \pi_l > \pi_{l,e}.$$

We can rewrite (13) as

(13′) $$\pi(p_m p_m) - \pi(p_m p_e) > \pi_l(p_e)/2$$

where $p_e$ replaces $p_D$ in the second term since we allow the incumbent to offer a discounted price as low as the duopoly price and where $\pi_l(p_e)$ equals $\pi_{E,e} + \pi_{l,e}$.

The inequality in (13′) will clearly hold whenever upstream competition takes the Bertrand form since, in that case, upstream duopoly profits are zero. As the duopoly price increases, the left hand side of (13′) decreases while the right hand side increases. Thus, at the other extreme, the inequality in (13′) will clearly not hold if the entrant and the incumbent can collude perfectly since the duopoly price equals the monopoly price. Given this, there must be some price $p^*$ such that if $p_e < p^*$, then the incumbent can use an exclusive contract that decreases welfare to deter entry even when the entrant is allowed to make side payments to a buyer who refuses to sign the exclusive contract. That is, exclusive contracts are more likely to deter entry as upstream duopoly competition becomes more intense. Thus, while the ability of the entrant to make side payments in period 1 limits the ability of the monopolist to deter entry, it does so precisely in those situations where entry contributes the least to social welfare.

Moreover, as we show in the next section, if long-term contracts are available, then entrant side payments no longer limit the ability of exclusive contracts to deter entry.

V.  Long-Term Contracts

In the two-period model described in section II, the incumbent monopolist is able to use its power over period 1 prices to induce downstream firms to pay it a monopoly price in period 2. In that model, the exclusive contract has this effect because of our assumption about the technology.  If the entrant could not make any sales in period 1, the entrant could not compete on an equal footing with the incumbent in period 2.  Thus, by signing exclusive contracts with the incumbent in period 1, downstream firms committed themselves to pay the incumbent a monopoly price in period 2.  In this section, we show that we can relax this assumption about technology if we assume instead that firms can sign long-term contracts in period 1 that set the period 2 price.

Consider a two period model in which an incumbent monopolist is the only seller in period 1 and an entrant can enter in period 2.  Suppose that both firms can sign long-term contracts before the start of period 1 that would commit them to sell at a set price in period 2.  In this case, the results in section II guarantee that an incumbent monopolist can still use exclusive contracts to deter entry.  To see this, recall that the incumbent selects his discount by working back from the period 2 duopoly state.  Allowing the entrant to commit to some price in period 2 forces the period 2 duopoly price lower and forces the incumbent to offer a larger discount. However, since we have shown that the incumbent can profitably use discounted exclusive contracts to deter entry for any period 2 duopoly price, the incumbent can still use exclusive contracts to deter entry.

As mentioned in the introduction, this type of contract has characteristics of a tying contract where the tied product is the same product purchased in the next period. The same reasoning, of course, would apply if the incumbent were an un-threatened monopolist in one input and faced competition for a second input, both of which are used by downstream competitors. Thus, downstream competition also provides an anticompetitive explanation for tying contracts.

This same insight also shows that the incumbent's strategy of bribing a downstream firm not to sign an exclusive contract (or a tying contract) will not work when the incumbent can sign long term contracts. The incumbent can costlessly guarantee marginal cost pricing in a duopoly market with the following contract. It offers a downstream firm a discount for signing an exclusive contract and promises it a second period price equal to marginal cost unless the incumbent can show that both downstream firms signed this contract. Thus, if the entrant does induce a buyer not to sign the exclusive, it can enter but will not earn any profits in the second period. So, it is not willing to pay a positive bribe to a buyer who does not sign the exclusive contract. We are now in the basic two period model where duopoly prices are Bertrand prices, so Proposition 1 applies. Of course, the discount the incumbent must offer increases, which reduces the anti-competitive impact of the exclusive (or tying) contract. But, when the buyers do compete downstream, the discount will not have to equal the Bertrand price, so there is still some anticompetitive impact.

## V. Conclusion

_____The basic model presented in this paper relies on three assumptions: an incumbent monopolist sells to competing downstream firms; an entrant can not initially supply a buyer at the same cost as the incumbent; and this entrant can supply buyers at the same cost as the incumbent if it can make some sales during an interim period to at least one firm. Where these assumptions hold, this paper shows that an incumbent monopolist can profitably deter entry by offering discounts to firms that sign exclusive contracts. Where the incumbent monopolist can offer a long-term exclusive contract, this paper shows that an incumbent monopolist can deter future entry even when the entrant does not need to make sales during the interim period in order to compete later on an equal footing with the incumbent.

The anticompetitive harm that results from such an exclusionary strategy depends on several factors. As the time required for entry decreases, the incumbent monopolist will need to offer downstream firms progressively larger discounts. Thus, the anticompetitive harm from this exclusionary strategy decreases as the length of the interim period decreases. As the intensity of downstream competition lessens, we believe that the incumbent monopolist will need to offer downstream firms progressively larger discounts to get them to sign the exclusive contracts. If we are correct, then the anticompetitive harm from this exclusionary strategy will also decrease as downstream competition decreases.

In some cases involving a single entrant, the entrant can counter the incumbent monopolist's use of exclusive contracts simply by compensating a downstream firm for its losses during the interim period. In other cases involving a single entrant, this will not be the case.

Finally, we want to stress that since exclusive contracts can help induce efficient investments

(see Segal and Whinston (2000b)), we are certainly not advocating a *per se* rule against exclusive

contracts. In some cases, even where exclusive contracts deter entry, these efficiency benefits

may outweigh any anticompetitive harm from the use of exclusive contracts.

## References

Aghion, Phillippe and Bolton, Patrick. "Contracts as a Barrier to Entry." *American Economic Review*, June 1987, 77(3), pp. 388-401.

Bernheim, B. Douglas, and Whinston, Michael D., "Exclusive Dealing." *Journal of Political Economy*, February 1998, 106(1), pp. 64-103.

Bork, Robert H., *The Antitrust Paradox*, New York: Basic Books, 1978.

Innes, Robert, and Richard J. Sexton, "Strategic Buyers and Exclusionary Contracts," *American Economic Review*, June 1994, 84(3), pp. 566-84.

Posner, Richard A., *Antitrust Law: An Economic Perspective*, Chicago: University of Chicago Press, 1976.

Rasmusen, Eric B., Ramseyer, J. Mark and Wiley, John Shepard Jr., "Naked Exclusion." *American Economic Review*, December 1991, 81(5), pp. 1137-45.

Segal, Ilya R. and Whinston, Michael D. "Naked Exclusion and Buyer Coordination." *American Economic Review*, March 2000a, 90(1) pp. 296-309.

------. "Exclusive Contracts and Protection of Investments." *The RAND Journal of Economics*, Winter 2000b, 31(4), pp. 603-33.